IMAGES OF WAR

D-DAY TO VICTORY

IMAGES OF WAR

D-DAY TO VICTORY

Maureen Hill

Photographs by the Daily Mail

MARKS & SPENCER

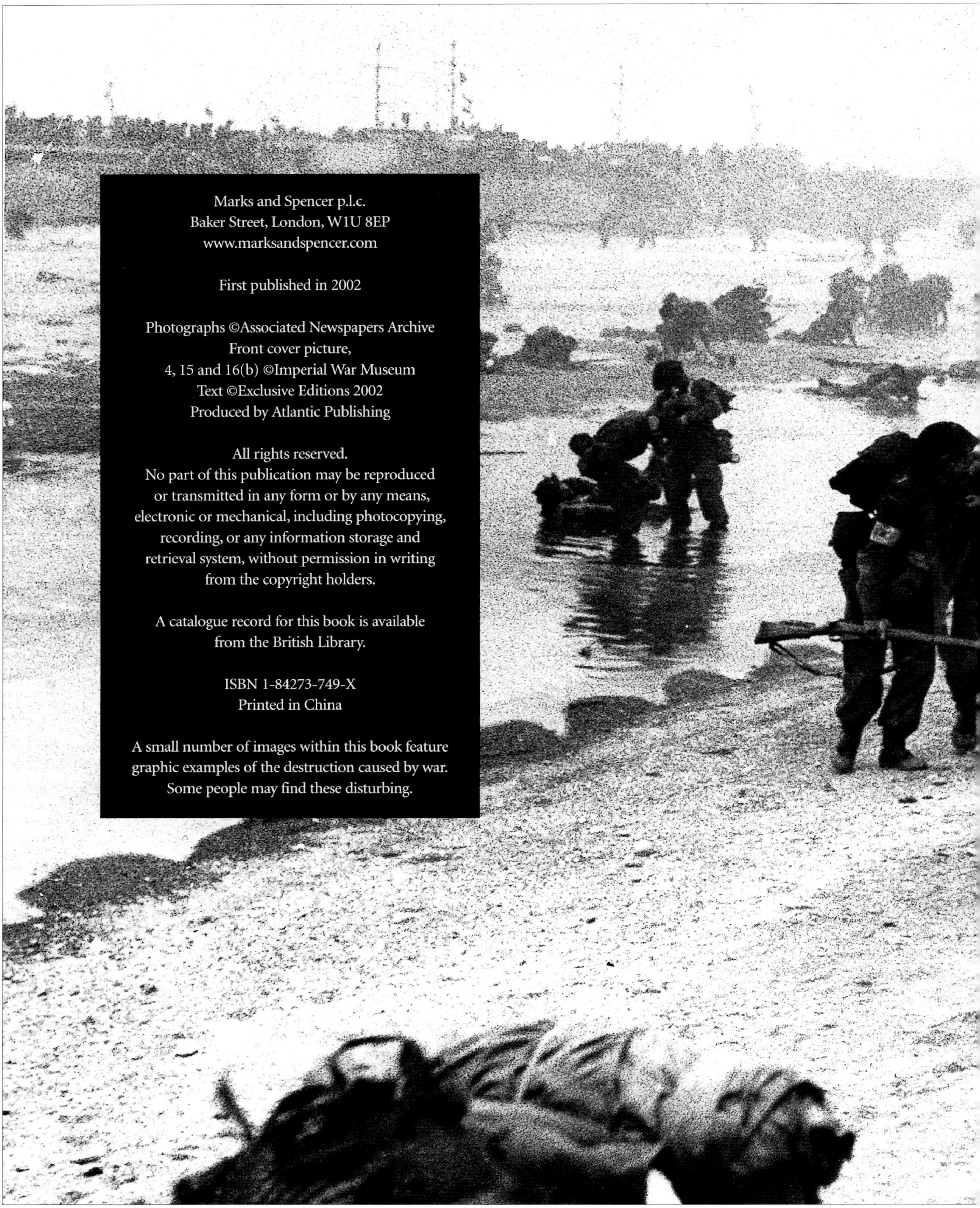

Marks and Spencer p.l.c.
Baker Street, London, W1U 8EP
www.marksandspencer.com

First published in 2002

Produced by Atlantic Publishing

A catalogue record for this book is available
from the British Library.

ISBN 1-84273-749-X
Printed in China

A small number of images within this book feature
graphic examples of the destruction caused by war.
Some people may find these disturbing.

Introduction

War throughout the world

When war broke out in September 1939 few people imagined that it would be virtually another six years before the peace would be restored. The public was not naïve enough to think that it would be over quickly. It was only a quarter of a century since the outbreak of the 'Great War' in August 1914, which most then believed would be 'over by Christmas'.

During those six years the Second World War developed in many ways. There were many different phases, marked by varying military strategies on both sides and, as the years went by, a variety of different fronts opened. The conflict which began as one focused on Western Europe grew to encompass the globe, as two of the largest and most powerful nations, the United States of America and the Soviet Union, were drawn in, but for almost a year Britain, aided by her colonies, fought alone.

The British Expeditionary Force (BEF), sent to Europe almost as soon as war was declared, became bogged down in the 'Phoney War' in which neither side made any real military moves on land, although the Royal Navy was engaged in sea battles in the Atlantic. When the Germans attacked Norway, Denmark, the Low Countries and France in April 1940, the BEF was pushed back to the beaches of Dunkirk by late May 1940. The dramatic rescue of the majority of the men enabled the newly installed Prime Minister, Winston Churchill, to turn what could have been an ignominious defeat into a triumph of the British Spirit.

Mainland Europe became a fortress and Britain, while it had the manpower, did not have the equipment with which to mount an attack. Germany tried to press home its advantage by preparing for an invasion of Britain. During the 'Battle of Britain' the Luftwaffe and the RAF fought for air supremacy to ensure invading troopships could either be attacked or defended. It was a battle won by the RAF and Germany resorted to aerial bombardment of British towns and cities in an attempt to destroy the means of weapons production and to demoralise the population in order that they would encourage the government to sue for peace.

From the fall of France in June 1940 to Germany's attack on the Soviet Union in June 1941, was perhaps the darkest hour for Britain. Faced with the fear of invasion, the Blitz and the fact that it had no military allies, it was a bleak year. By the end of 1941, not only was the Soviet Union an ally but the USA, which had offered economic and moral support from the beginning, had been drawn into the fighting when Japan attacked its fleet at Pearl Harbor in December of that year.

American troops landed in Britain in January 1942 to help fight the war in Europe. By this time there was fighting throughout the world: in Africa, the Far East, the Pacific and the Soviet Union; but it was to be more than two years before an attempt could be made to attack Hitler's 'Fortress Europe'. The D-Day landings in June 1944 were only the 'beginning of the end'. Victory in Europe came in May 1945 but it was to be a further three months and victory over Japan before the conflict was finally ended.

This book focuses on the period from D-Day, and the push through Europe, to Berlin and the defeat of Nazism. The images, drawn from the impressive archive of the *Daily Mail*, have been restored to original condition. They chart the difficulties faced by the Allies in what had been Germany's stronghold of the European mainland, showing both the misery and cruelty of war, and the growing optimism which found its peak in the delighted outpourings of VE Day, and later VJ Day.

Long road to Victory

The entry of America into the war had a variety of consequences for Britain. The increased number of troops and weapons to call on made the prospect of defeating Hitler more of a reality but it meant that a new theatre of war opened in the Pacific. And while Britain had a new and powerful military ally, Germany also gained an ally in Japan, to add to its alliance with Mussolini's Italy, in an alignment termed the Axis Powers.

Initially, the Axis Powers made advances on several fronts. In North Africa Britain's Eighth Army suffered defeats at the hands of Rommel's Afrika Korps, which emphasised Axis superiority in the Mediterranean where Malta was besieged as a threat to German and Italian supply lines. On the Eastern Front the Allies' other main constituent, the Soviet Red Army, was locked in severe fighting with the Germans. The Japanese pressed home their advantage in the Pacific with lightning strikes which saw the fall of Hong Kong and Singapore as well as the establishment of Japanese rule in many of the sovereign countries of South-East Asia, from Burma to the Philippines. Britain and America's main response was aerial bombing. US bombers, operating from aircraft carriers, hit Tokyo but in Europe much more severe bombing raids took place on Germany. Air Marshal 'Bomber' Harris organised devastating raids, including a 1000-bomber attack on Cologne.

Success for the Allies in the Mediterranean brought about the surrender of Italy on 8th September, 1943. This was made possible by the victory of the Eighth Army, under its new commander General Montgomery, at El Alamein in North Africa. On 15th November church bells rang throughout Britain for the first time since the beginning of the war. The ringing of church bells was supposed to signal an invasion but on this occasion they rang to celebrate the El Alamein success. The Eighth Army fought on and in May 1943 110,000 German and 40,000 Italian soldiers capitulated, bringing an end to the North Africa campaign. The victory secured a base from which the Allies could mount an assault on Italy, firstly taking the islands of Lampedusa, Pantelleria and Sicily before landing on the mainland to force the fall of Mussolini and the country's surrender. However, while Italy laid down its arms, its recent ally, Germany, did not and retained control of Rome for more than a year.

1943 marked a real turning point in the war. On the Eastern Front there were critical losses for Germany. Stalingrad was taken by the Red Army which continued to push the Germans back across most of the front, engaging in fierce fighting, including a massive tank battle around the city of Kursk in July. Elsewhere Germany was losing superiority in many areas – U-boats were losing their ability to move undetected and harry shipping in the Atlantic and, in the Ruhr, RAF planes had breached two major dams causing severe damage to Germany's major industrial area.

At the very end of 1943 it was announced that the American general, Dwight D. Eisenhower, was to be the supreme commander of the Allies' operation to invade Europe from the west. He was to work with General Montgomery – both Ike and Monty, as they were nicknamed, were successful veterans of the North African campaigns. The invasion was to be a difficult and dangerous undertaking as despite Germany's defeats on other fronts, it had a secure border on the coasts of western Europe.

An attempt to land troops by sea on the French coast had been made in August 1942. More than 6000 soldiers drawn from British, American, Canadian and Free French divisions, supported by air and naval cover, landed at Dieppe. Fighting lasted nine hours before the Allies were overwhelmed. Losses from the raid were high – more than a thousand men dead and 2500 taken prisoner, with tremendous losses of heavy equipment including invasion barges, tanks, troop and attack ships and almost 100 Allied aircraft. The operation, headed by Admiral Lord Louis Mountbatten, was deemed to have been disastrous but was claimed to have been only a reconnaissance mission and not an attempt at a full-scale invasion.

Whatever its purpose the Dieppe raid gave the Allies valuable lessons in what would be required in an all-out attack on Hitler's Fortress Europe. Eisenhower and the commanders at Allied Supreme Command used the experience when preparing the strategy for the D-Day landings. By April 1944 Britain had become a gigantic armed camp with British, American and Commonwealth troops as well as remnants of European armies such as the Free French and the Poles, stationed throughout the country. Along the length of southern Britain large-scale military exercises were under way, with troops practising coastal assault techniques.

Everyone knew the invasion was imminent but clearly the best way to ensure maximum protection for the first wave of troops was to maintain an element of surprise. Visitors were banned from going within 10 miles of the coast from Land's End to The Wash to help maintain secrecy on the Allies' training plans. In March travel to Eire had been banned to try to prevent information being passed to diplomats in enemy consulates in Dublin. This ban was followed in April by a restriction on all foreign diplomats in London, who were prevented from travelling and from sending dispatches without inspection. Further measures to maintain secrecy were the use of decoy ships and forces to suggest concentrations of troops and equipment in a variety of different areas so that the German High Command could not be sure when or where the attack might come.

D-Day came on the morning of 6th June 1944. In the early dawn light troop barges came ashore on the beaches of Normandy. British and Canadian forces landed at beaches codenamed Gold, Juno and Sword to the north of the port of Caen. US troops landed further west, closer to the Cherbourg Peninsula at Utah and Omaha beaches. The invading troops came under heavy fire but the Germans had been taken by surprise, believing that the invasion would come in the Pas de Calais, farther east. Considering the Normandy manoeuvres to be a bluff to draw the defences the German High Command maintained their presence in north-eastern France.

The less heavily defended Normandy coast was further bolstered as a landing place by heavy bombing of rail links and bridges in the area prior to D-Day. This meant that Germany found it difficult to move troops and supplies to the front. Immediately before the sea-borne landing, from midnight to 5.30 a.m. parachutists and gliders had landed behind enemy lines to take key points by surprise. The combination of these factors made Operation Overlord, as the landings were codenamed, a success from day one. By midnight on June 6th the Allies had moved several miles inland across a broad front, having landed 155,000 men for a loss of 9000.

In the following days building on the success of D-

Day was an immense undertaking. Not only were the Allies engaged in ferocious fighting for virtually every inch of land, especially around Cherbourg, but it was necessary to establish supply lines from Britain. Artificial, or Mulberry, harbours were constructed off the Normandy coast to allow ships to dock to unload more troops and supplies. Six days after the initial landings the various Allied divisions had linked their beachheads to establish a broad front which pushed through Normandy, to be refreshed and supplemented by new troops from Britain.

By the end of July the German resistance in Normandy was broken. The failure of the German High Command to be able to re-supply the divisions in Normandy with either men or equipment due to Allied air strikes on the supply routes, together with the overwhelming strength of the Allied troops, meant that despite the ferocious defence by some German soldiers they were unable to defeat the odds. The fall of the Norman town of Caen allowed the Allies a clear route to Paris, which was liberated amid emotional scenes of celebration and retribution on 25th August, 1944.

Throughout the remaining months of 1944 and the first few months of 1945, the Allies made real progress. A second front was opened in France when Free French troops led an assault on the beaches between Nice and Marseille on 15th August 1944. The Soviet Red Army was pushing westward, freeing the countries of eastern Europe from German occupation. By 20th October 1944 the first city in Germany had fallen to the Allies. At the same time in the Pacific, the Allies, spearheaded by the Americans, were making progress in regaining ground in areas like the Philippines. Fighting on this front was particularly fierce, the Japanese suicide, or kamikaze, pilots symbolic of the zeal with which the Japanese military prosecuted the war.

The push through Europe on both the Eastern and Western Fronts was not without its problems. A daring attempt to shorten the war was devised by General Eisenhower. Airborne troops were dropped behind enemy lines to try to seize the bridges at Nijmegen, Grave and Arnhem on the lower Rhine. Two bridges were taken but the third at Arnhem proved too difficult, and after eight days of fighting against overwhelming odds the Allies pulled back. Three months later, in December 1944, the German army managed to break through the Allied lines in the Ardennes. The resulting action was dubbed the Battle of the Bulge.

By mid-January the Ardennes line was re-secured and the Allies continued their push towards Germany. On 24th March 1945 the Western Allies crossed the Rhine which had been a major line of defence for the Germans. In the following weeks many of the German concentration camps were revealed and Allied resources went into trying to relieve the suffering and save lives, often to no avail, as the people incarcerated there had been treated so appallingly that they were too weak to survive. Evidence was also uncovered of a deliberate plan to kill all Jews that came under the Nazi sphere of influence. This genocide, Hitler's 'Final Solution', led to the deaths of six million men, women and children, most in gas chambers specially constructed for this singularly evil purpose.

Devastating bombing raids on major German cities like Dresden and Berlin supported the ground troops' efforts as they pushed on towards the capital. The Red Army was the first of the Allies to reach Berlin and as they stormed through the city Hitler committed suicide on April 30th. The war in Europe was all but over. On 7th May, General Jodl signed the instrument of unconditional surrender.

The following day, 8th May, was pronounced Victory in Europe Day. There were joyous scenes throughout Britain; it was a time for parties and thanksgiving with London a focus for the celebrations. During the day Buckingham Palace became a centre for the festivities. Crowds gathered to cheer the King and Queen on the Palace balcony; they were joined by other members of the Royal Family, including Princesses Elizabeth and Margaret, as well as by Prime Minister Winston Churchill. As night fell the crowd moved down The Mall to Trafalgar Square and Piccadilly Circus where a more unrestrained party took place until the small hours of the morning.

VE Day only marked the end of one major phase of the war. There was still Japan to defeat in the Far East. Many British troops, freed from the fighting in Europe, were transferred to the Pacific. Japan fought ferociously to retain every inch of land it had occupied and the battles in the Pacific were costly in terms of soldiers, lives lost. A decision was made by the Allies to try to hasten the surrender of Japan by using a newly-developed weapon of unimagined power – the atom bomb. On August 6th the city of Hiroshima was destroyed by one such bomb. The dropping of a second bomb three days later on the city of Nagasaki brought about Japan's unconditional surrender.

VJ Day on 14th August 1945 was celebrated with scenes similar to those just three months earlier for VE Day. This time people could rejoice in the knowledge that the war was finally over.

Once the celebrations were over it was time to turn to face the peace. Across the world 55 million people had lost their lives and many ancient and powerful cities lay in ruins. Everyone had to face the task of rebuilding: rebuilding the material world, rebuilding relationships fractured by war, rebuilding nations and national consciousness. There was also much for the world and its people to come to terms with: the unleashing of the most devastating and dangerous weapon ever seen; the separation of Eastern and Western Europe; and the knowledge and understanding of the amazing inhumanity that can flourish in fear and war.

Allied armada

Opposite: Official shots of the 'greatest armada the world has ever seen', as it crossed the English Channel in the early hours of 6th June 1944. The wing of the RAF plane from which the photograph was taken is visible *top* and the French coast can just be made out in the top right *below*.

Right: American army preparations for D-Day on Slapton Sands, Devon. 749 GIs were killed when one of these training exercises went horribly wrong. In order to give the troops 'battle experience' live rounds were used and unwittingly the soldiers killed many of their comrades.

Below: A 'duck' is loaded onto a transport carrier by American 'amphibious' troops. These vehicles functioned on both water and land, enabling troops to disembark at sea, navigate to shore and then convert to a land cruiser.

Going ashore

Opposite: Not all troop transport landed soldiers on the beaches, most had to wade ashore carrying all their equipment from barges or smaller ships.

Right: Loading the last pieces of equipment before setting off to join the invading armada out in the Channel. This small photograph emphasises the planning and logistics of Operation Overlord in which not only the troops had to be transported across the Channel, but all the weapons, vehicles and equipment needed, together with systems to help feed and support the soldiers.

Below: American GIs huddle behind the protection of the walls of the landing craft as it approaches the beachhead on the coast of France. Onshore can be seen smoke from shells from naval gunfire used to support the landing. It highlights the dangers of those early landings when not only were there risks from German air and shore batteries, but there were dangers from 'friendly fire'.

Sword Beach

Below: After the initial landings on Sword Beach, round the port of Ouistreham, British troops prepare to move off the beach and push inland towards Caen. Sword was the most easterly of the landing beaches; British troops also landed at beaches codenamed Juno and Gold near Arromanches and Courseulles.

Right: American troops, carrying full equipment, wade ashore. The American landing beaches, codenamed Omaha and Utah, were farther west than the British and Canadian landing points. Troops moved out into the Cherbourg Peninsula as well as pressing south.

Opposite top: GIs landing at one of the American beachheads. Stretching into the distance is a line of troops moving inland.

Opposite below: A picture taken on D-Day+1 as British infantry and Red Cross personnel come ashore.

View from the air

Right: A view from an American aircraft on the morning of D-Day. From the air the pattern of movement can be seen: the large ships, as well as the smaller landing craft, the dots of men and finally the vehicles which move off the beach to attack inland.

Above: The scene on the beach on D-Day after the initial landings. Barbed wire was only a minor hazard of the German shore defences. Mines were the major problem and the beaches had to be cleared before the troops landed. The low tide on 6th June provided an opportunity to do this job effectively.

Opposite: Taken during a training exercise just before D-Day this photograph shows some of the equipment needed for the landings. The barrage balloon offers some protection from enemy aircraft and here army engineers are practising with slat and wire temporary road surfaces to enable vehicles to move over the soft, fine sands of the Normandy coast.

US525
US320
320

First prisoners

Above: Early on, in the first days of the invasion, the Allies began to take prisoners. Here a German soldier surrenders to the Americans.

Right: Captured on D-Day+1 these German prisoners are marched by British soldiers through a French village under the gaze of the local inhabitants.

Opposite top: The scene on the beach in the first few days after the landings - unloading supplies, in this case the wooden slat and wire runners that were essential to get the vehicles moving.

Opposite below: A beachhead scene in the early days of the invasion. Troops and equipment are moving out. On the ridge are the field hospital tents dealing with the wounded and the barrage balloon offers some protection from air attack.

Wounded prisoners

Above: Fellow German soldiers carry their wounded comrade to an evacuation barge just 8 days after D-Day. At this stage troops were still being landed from Britain and the ships which delivered them were busy taking POWs back to detention camps.

Right: Two injured POWs, guarded by an American Military Policeman, wait in a jeep as a 'duck', an amphibious vehicle, passes through a liberated village. It is D-Day+4 and already the tricolour flies from the public building on the left.

Opposite: When the town of Ste Mère-Eglise, inland from Utah beach, was captured after fierce fighting, this German sniper was taken prisoner. Here he rides to captivity on the bumper of an American jeep.

HQ-

The price of war

Opposite top: The main street of the town of Isigny, famed in peacetime for the quality of its dairy produce. Lying between the two American beachheads, the town was attacked by both sides from the air, from the sea and by fighting on land but was liberated within the first few days of the invasion.

Opposite below: A grim scene from June 1944 in the once quiet Normandy town of Pont l'Abb. Carrying all they have managed to salvage from their wrecked homes, these women and children hurry past a German military vehicle and its driver, killed in the Allied advance.

Above: These young German soldiers claimed to be 18 years old but look little more than 14 or 15. They wait with other POWs to be shipped back to England for internment less than a week after D-Day.

Left: A Nazi officer, decorated with the Iron Cross, captured in the Cherbourg Peninsula, ponders the fate of the Germans in northern France.

Come out with your hands up!

Opposite top: While the Allies were beginning the assault on the Germans in northern France, fighting continued in Italy. An attack at Anzio in January 1944 was the beginning of an attempt to force German troops out of the parts of Italy they still occupied after the defeat of Mussolini. By June the Allies were making good progress. Here a German soldier holed up in a dug-out in Piedmont waves a flag of surrender.

Opposite below: Polish troops capture a German soldier as he emerges from his hiding place.

Right: In the French town of Carentan, liberated by the Americans in the second week of the invasion, volunteers from the fire department begin the work of reconstruction.

Below: Ironically this is a French anti-tank unit rolling through the Italian town of Bolsena on 14th June, just as many of their compatriots in France are being liberated by others of the Allies.

Bastille Day 1944

Opposite top left: The town of Bayeux celebrates Bastille Day, liberated after four years of German occupation. It was the largest crowd ever seen in the town, many people having travelled from the nearby town of Caen which had suffered terrible damage in the fighting. Crowds were also swelled by Allied troops and, as the accompanying caption iterated, 'members of the Maquis who, but a few hours before, had been fighting behind the German lines'.

Opposite top right: Another scene in Bayeux on Bastille Day but this time with a reminder that the liberation struggle is not over. As the people celebrate, tanks roll past on their way to the front.

Opposite below: British troops play a celebratory football match against a local French team.

Right: The Curé of Caen walks amidst the ruins of the town while German shelling continues.

Below: German prisoners from the Cherbourg Peninsula are marched through the streets of the city by American forces.

CHARCUTERIE
DU CENTRE

Seeking refuge

Right: The main street of the small town of Creully in Normandy with American and British troops alongside local inhabitants on their way to Mass. The caption accompanying this photograph draws attention to a growing problem in July 1944 - refugees. By this time only part of France had been liberated and large numbers of people from behind the German lines fled to liberated towns like that pictured here.

Below: Three German prisoners being marched out of the industrial town of Colombelles which fell after heavy bombardment from the air.

Opposite top left: These German artillery engineers, captured near Caen, were originally stationed at Dieppe before being sent to fight as infantry.

Opposite top right: An eighteen-year-old sniper surrenders after being wounded.

Opposite below: A boy of fourteen captured in Coutances after sniping at American soldiers.

Paratroopers mark opening of a second front in France

Opposite top: Paratroopers land in southern France to herald an Allied beachhead landing on a 100-mile coastal strip from Nice to Marseille on the morning of 15th August 1944.

Opposite below: The town of St-Lô in Normandy in August 1944. The battle for the town was particularly fierce, the Germans mounting a strong defence, and by the time it was liberated there was hardly a building left standing in the centre.

Above: Two thousand German soldiers captured in the battle for Avranches are marched back to the town by the Americans.

Right: As the Allies pushed west from Normandy parts of Brittany were liberated. Here the citizens of Rennes come out to cheer the Americans as they enter the town.

August in Avranches

Right: In brilliant August sunshine American tanks, watched by the local people, rumble through the streets of Avranches.

Below: Canadian troops 'clean up' in May-sur-Orne as they search house-to-house for enemy soldiers.

Opposite top left: Mlle. Marie Jose Ruella, aged 74, refused to leave her home in the village of Amayé-sur-Orne despite the shelling and was the only person left to welcome the British troops as they passed through the village.

Opposite top right: A much-decorated German soldier is captured. His medals include: first and second class iron crosses, a wound badge, the Russian medal and a sharpshooter's medal.

Opposite below: A British Bren-gunner takes up position on the Caen-Vire road on the outskirts of the village of Jurques.

Time for a rest

Opposite: By the third week in August the Allies had been fighting for ten weeks and while in some areas German resistance was relatively light, in many the fighting was fierce. Here exhausted soldiers catch a few moments' sleep in the Normandy countryside.

Right: With the church spire left standing in the background, bulldozers get to work on clearing the rubble in the town of Aunay-sur-Odon. The Germans had made barriers out of the wreckage and the craters in order to try to stem the Allied advance.

Above: A road is cleared through the ruined town of Villers-Bocage. Craters have been filled in and obstructions removed so that convoys of troops and equipment can be moved to new forward areas.

Mont-St-Michel intact

Right: A jeep drives along the causeway to the world-famous landmark of Mont-St-Michel which the Germans had evacuated in early August as the American army pushed through into Brittany. The island and its buildings were undamaged.

Below: Farther east in the town of Falaise the buildings did not escape damage (as those in Mont-St-Michel). This is a view of the town taken after Canadian forces had liberated it.

Opposite top: Damaged German fighter planes at Le Bourget airport, Paris. As the Allies advanced on Paris the airport suffered both bombing by Allied aircraft and shelling by German guns attempting to stop the Allied advance.

Opposite below: Paris was liberated on 25th August amid scenes of both jubilation and retribution. Police had to protect many Germans from the fury of Parisians. Here Nazi prisoners, driven under the Eiffel Tower, face the jeers of the population.

Paris liberated

Right: A Parisian woman welcomes the liberating American soldiers with a kiss.

Below: German soldiers are rounded up in the streets of Paris. Once the Allies had broken out of Normandy, progress towards Paris was swift. Resistance elements managed to take the Préfecture when news came that the Allies were close. The first Allied troops to enter the city were the Free French, led by General Leclerc.

Opposite top: Parisians fall to the ground as German snipers, who had remained hidden for three days, target machine-gun fire at General de Gaulle as he arrives at Notre Dame for a Thanksgiving Service.

Opposite below: Civilians and troops celebrating the liberation.

BAZAR
DE L'HOTEL DE VILLE
BAZAR DE L'HOTEL DE VILLE
DE L'HOTEL DE VILLE
D'ARGENT
LA CHEMISE
D'ARGENT

Street fighting

Right: A group of GIs and a member of the Resistance work to flush out German snipers, barricaded in buildings in the Paris streets two days after the liberation.

Below: While elsewhere in the city Parisians celebrate, French troops fire at the remnants of the German army who have holed-up in defendable positions.

Opposite top left: At Place de la Concorde General de Gaulle takes the salute alongside the commanders of the US army divisions, and the commissioner of liberated France, while thousands of American troops with their equipment march down the Champs Élysées (*opposite below*).

Opposite top right: Food supplies were sent almost immediately to Paris by the Allies. Here British troops and local women chat alongside a lorry loaded with flour.

MP
MP
MP

CHURCHILLS PROMISE
FOOD FOR PARIS
VIVE LA FRANCE
VIVRES PO

Curses for the defeated

Right: A woman leans forward to curse this captured German soldier as he is marched at gunpoint through the streets of St-Mihiel in northern France.

Below: A German prisoner in Brest hands a 'safe conduct' pamphlet to Lt W. F. Kinney of Chicago. The pamphlets were shot over the German lines carrying a guarantee of good treatment to those who surrendered.

Opposite top: A photograph taken as the men from the Free French army move in to storm the Chamber of Deputies where around 500 German troops barricaded themselves as a last-ditch defence. They were eventually forced to surrender.

Opposite below: US soldiers and Resistance fighters sweep through the streets of Paris to clear out German snipers. Note the civilian woman pressing to the wall on the corner, and the spent cartridges that litter the street.

SAVART-LANGE

La Maison est ouverte
Mademoiselle Hortense

Rubble in Rouen

Opposite top: The delicate spire of Rouen Cathedral rises above the rubble left behind after the fierce fighting needed for the Allies to take the city.

Opposite below: The scene in the submarine pens at Brest as the town surrendered. It was from Brest that many of the German U-boats left to harry shipping in the North Atlantic.

Above: Tanks and guns cross a canal bridge built by British engineers as the Allies push into Holland.

Right: The people of Dieppe are able to see their beach again after four years of German occupation when the coastal area had been off-limits to civilians.

Allied airborne army lands in Holland

Above: Allied paratroopers pictured before taking off for the assault on German-occupied Holland in September, 1944.

Left: Waves of paratroopers drop from C-47 transport planes as part of an Allied airborne assault which was to have seized the bridges at Nijmegen, Grave and Arnhem and give the Allies control of the lower Rhine. However, after eight days of fierce fighting they were unable to secure Arnhem and, with losses of 7600 men dead or taken prisoner, had to pull back.

Opposite top: Later, in October, the Allies were able to make more progress in Holland. Here British troops advance along a ditch during an attack on the village of St Michielsgestel outside Hertogenbosch.

Opposite below: British troops advance cautiously across open countryside towards the town of Venray, an important road and rail junction.

Autumn advances

Right: Canadian troops walk down the Boulevard Pasteur in Calais which fell to the Allies on the first day of October. In the background is the clock tower which can be seen from Dover.

Below: American 4.2 mortar shells land in the small village of Le Tholy as the Allies move through northern France.

Opposite top: Farther east in Holland, Allied tanks advance through the streets of Schijndel, near Tilburg.

Opposite below: One minute after midnight on 22nd October, the British Second Army under General Dempsey started a drive for Hertogenbosch, a Dutch railway and communications centre vital to the Germans. Here infantry troops are pictured in a trench captured during the advance.

On the Italian Front

Right: In October and November the Allies were making advances in Italy as well as in France, Belgium and Holland. A battalion of the Durham Light Infantry had defeated the Germans guarding Bologna and other British and Canadian troops had liberated Cesena. Here Italian patriots search the town for remnants of the enemy.

Below: A shell explodes next to a soldier near Arnhem - miraculously he survived.

Opposite top: Polish soldiers take cover in a wrecked farmhouse, just 400 yards from the enemy line at Hooge Zwaluwe in Holland.

Opposite below: 'Rushing through Flushing'. British troops at the double as they move through the narrow streets of the Dutch town of Flushing on the look-out for enemy snipers.

V-rocket bomb falls in Belgian town

Opposite: 4th December 1944 and although the Germans are withdrawing they are still capable of mounting attacks on liberated towns by using pilotless V2 rocket bombs. Pictured here is the tragic and harrowing result of an attack on a Belgian town.

Right: Police hold back the crowds of Parisians who turned out to cheer Winston Churchill as he was granted the freedom of the city.

Below: British Bren-gunners keep a sharp look-out for enemy movements along the front line near the River Maas in Holland at the end of November.

Mercy train to St-Nazaire

Below: Women peep out of a train which is being handed over to Allied troops. They are among 13,000 civilians evacuated from the town of St-Nazaire which, in January 1945, was still held by the Germans.

Right and opposite below: German officers, Hauptmann D. Muller, and Oberleutnants Schultz-Koehn, Von Reibnitz and Jentzsch negotiate with French and American commanders to allow the evacuation of civilians from St-Nazaire. A train, empty save for two French nurses, was allowed into the town after being searched by the Germans, to pick up the townspeople. Negotiations took place at the station of Cordemais, halfway between Nantes and St-Nazaire, while the battle raged around it.

Opposite top: British troops hunting snipers in the streets of Blerick, a town on the River Maas, in December 1944. This marked the end of the German bridgehead on the western bank of the Maas.

The big three meet at Yalta

Right: British Prime Minister Winston Churchill shakes hands with the Soviet Union's Marshal Stalin, while US President Roosevelt looks on from his chair at a meeting of the three main Allied powers at Yalta in the Crimea. At this meeting in February 1945 plans were made to divide Germany into four zones, controlled by Britain, Russia, America and France and to establish post-war 'zones of influence'. More immediately plans were drawn up for the invasion of the Japanese mainland.

Below: The British Second Army on patrol in tanks in the Dutch town of Susteren.

Opposite top: British 'buffaloes' transport men and supplies to Canadian troops who are advancing towards the Rhine in the flooded country round Nijmegen and Cleves.

Opposite below: Winston Churchill crosses the Rhine in an American craft, accompanied by Field Marshal Montgomery.

2D

Across the Rhine

Above: Rhona Churchill, war correspondent with the *Daily Mail*, was the first woman to cross the Rhine. Here she is accompanied by Winston Churchill and Field Marshal Montgomery on 25th March, 1945. Montgomery had crossed the Rhine at midnight on the 24th in amphibious craft, backed by air attack, a 2000-gun bombardment and two airborne paratroop divisions. Earlier in the day, further south at Remagen a platoon of American soldiers had spotted a rail bridge left intact by the Germans and managed to cross it and hold it until backed-up by reinforcements.

Right: The ruins of the German town of Julich, west of the Rhine, were shown to Winston Churchill when he visited the troops in Germany at the beginning of March.

Opposite: General Eisenhower and Field Marshal Montgomery had established their headquarters in Julich and here, outside the citadel, Winston Churchill is pictured with Monty and an American commander.

Building bridges

Right: An aerial view of the US First Army trucks and equipment rolling across a pontoon bridge on the Rhine. As they had done elsewhere the retreating German army destroyed virtually all of the bridges across the Rhine. It was necessary for the bridges to be replaced as quickly as possible and this was one of the areas where the skills of the engineers came to prominence.

Below: A view from the ground of men and supplies crossing the Rhine. There were of course numerous bridges built - this one was functioning a day after the Rhine had been first crossed by the Allies.

Opposite top: Earlier in the month Winston Churchill, on his visit to the Command HQ at Julich, walked over a Bailey bridge across the Roer, announcing, 'After the magnificent job your troops did getting across, it will be an honour to walk its length.'

Opposite below: Paratroopers of the First Airborne Division drop on the eastern banks of the Rhine from C-47 transport carriers. Photographed here is a fraction of the 40,000 men dropped in this mission.

YOU ARE NOW
CROSSING THE
RHINE RIVER
THROUGH COURTESY
OF 'E' CO. 17 ARMD.
ENGR. BN. AND
'C' CO. 202
ENGR. C. BN.

Rhine bridge constructed in six and a half hours

Opposite top: This pontoon bridge across the Rhine was constructed in the record time of six and a half hours.

Opposite below: Infantrymen of the US Seventh Army provide cover from the west bank of the Rhine for Allies crossing the river under fire from the Germans on the eastern bank.

Right: April 1945 and these British and Commonwealth soldiers held prisoner in Oflag 79 near Brunswick are liberated by the US army after being detained for five years.

Below: Men of the Seaforth Highlanders sweep through the Dutch town of Uelzen clearing houses of enemy snipers.

April brings release for thousands of POWs

Right: An American soldier is held aloft by Russian prisoners when Stalag 326-6K south-east of Munster was liberated. 30,000 Russian prisoners died in this camp from starvation and other privations.

Below: British soldiers from a camp near Brunswick cheer their release. Most of the men here were captured in the blitzkreig of 1940 when Germany swept through western Europe, pushing the British Expeditionary Force back to the beaches at Dunkirk.

Opposite top: Some of the 18,000 POWs at the Altengrabow Camp waiting for their release.

Opposite below: British POWs suffering from malnutrition are pictured here at Stalag 11B just south of Fallingbostel. It was the first POW camp housing British prisoners to be liberated.

The horrors of Belsen

Opposite: As the Second Army advanced in April 1945 the concentration camp at Belsen was captured. What they saw there shocked them and the world. Of the 60,000 civilians crammed into the camp most were suffering from typhus, typhoid and dysentery. Hundreds of people were dying daily despite the best efforts of Allied medical teams rushed to the camp. SS guards who had been in charge of the inmates were kept on at the camp to bury the dead.

Belsen was only one of many such camps in which Jewish people, and others whom the Nazi regime saw as polluting the Aryan purity of Germany, were incarcerated under conditions of terrible inhumanity – forced labour, starvation, disease and torture. As part of Hitler's 'Final Solution', the camps became the focus of genocide, an attempt to exterminate the Jewish race within Nazi occupied territory.

Above: Troops from the Third US Army move through the Czechoslovakian town of Asch in search of enemy snipers.

Left: Liberated British prisoners at Stalag 11B read the newspapers, anxious for news from home.

Berlin falls

Opposite: A Russian Red Army infantryman pictured in Berlin after a bitter battle which left more than 100,000 Germans dead and the city a smoking mass of ruins. In the last three weeks in April the Allies took over a million German soldiers prisoner. On the last day of April and with the Russians closing in on the Chancellery, Hitler committed suicide, as a final acknowledgement of Germany's defeat.

Above: Crowds gather in the Mall outside Buckingham Palace to cheer the King and Queen and the two princesses on VE Day. After Hitler's death it was a week before General Jodl signed Germany's unconditional surrender.

Right: VE Day, 8th May 1945, and people dance in Fleet Street amid the paper thrown from the offices of the major British newspapers.

'Today is VE Day!'

Right: Winston Churchill with members of the cabinet on the balcony of the Ministry of Health building from where he announced that Tuesday, 8th May 1945 was VE Day - Victory in Europe Day, for across the globe, in the Pacific, the war against Japan continued.

Above: In streets up and down Britain the flags came out and the people partied in the street.

Opposite: In Salisbury Square a family party celebrate with V for Victory signs, flags and streamers made from the tickertape that fed the news to newspaper offices in Fleet Street.

PAPER RAGS BONES
SUPPORT YOUR
SAVINGS
GROUP
WHITBREAD'S ALE & STOUT
DEWARS

Contrasting cities

Left: The ruins of the Reichstag, the building which housed the German Parliament, in June 1945.

Below: The streets at the heart of Berlin lie wrecked. Most of the damage was caused by RAF and American Airforce bombing raids in an attempt to destroy defensive positions and offer protection to the ground troops who entered the city in April.

Opposite: Piccadilly Circus at the heart of London jammed with crowds awaiting the official announcement of VE Day. The famous figure of Eros lies protected for the duration behind the boards covered in hoardings encouraging support for savings groups.

DLON HOTEL
Маршал Советского Союза
И. В. Сталин

VALTER LANGE
ebensmittel
74

Russians in Berlin

Left: On traffic duty at the Brandenburg Gate is a 22-year-old Russian woman soldier, Feodora Bondenko, who had marched from Kiev with Marshal Zhukov's forces.

Below: At a bend in the Kurfürstendamm, in front of the Kaiserin Augusta Gedächtniskirche scarred by Allied bombing, two Berlin women pass by a Russian signpost.

Opposite top: A huge portrait of Josef Stalin hangs outside the Adlon Hotel on Unter den Linden. By the time this photograph was taken in July 1945 it was known that Russia was to occupy almost half of Germany and a sector of Berlin.

Opposite below: A crowd of Berliners wait for a bus in a street just off Potsdamer Platz. Buses were one of the few ways for citizens to get around the city but the service was severely curtailed.

Life for the defeated citizens was harsh. They had to set about trying to clear up the wreckage, and in this photograph much rubble and a damaged vehicle still litter the street, but food, clean water and shelter were all in short supply.

Churchill meets Truman

Right: In July 1945 the three major Allied powers met again at Potsdam in an attempt to sort out the fine details of the peace process in Europe. The handshake here is the first meeting of Prime Minister Churchill with Harry S. Truman, the new American President. Tragically, President Roosevelt had died unexpectedly on 12th April 1945, less than a month before Germany's unconditional surrender and as Vice-President, Truman was sworn in.

Below: On a visit to Berlin Churchill rests in a chair that was said to have been in the bunker in which Hitler committed suicide.

Opposite: Churchill met British military commanders at Berlin airport when he arrived for the Potsdam conference which started on 15th July. The conference continued until the end of the month but by that time Churchill was no longer British Prime Minister. Immediately after the victory against Germany, the coalition government he had led since 1940 was dissolved and a new election called. Churchill's Conservative party suffered a shock defeat as Labour won a landslide victory in a country eager for change. The Labour Prime Minister, Clement Attlee, replaced Churchill at Potsdam.

VJ Day

Right: A London policeman is held aloft by military men from the US and New Zealand in celebration of VJ Day. Victory over Japan was bought at a terrible cost - the dropping of two atomic bombs, one on Hiroshima on 6th August, a second on Nagasaki three days later. On 14th August, 1945 Emperor Hirohito offered Japan's unconditional surrender, signalling the end to almost exactly six years of war.

Below: Service men and women celebrate in Piccadilly.

Opposite top: The Royal Family acknowledge the cheering crowds from the balcony of Buckingham Palace.

Opposite below: People throng the streets on 11th August as news of the defeat, if not surrender, of Japan filters through.

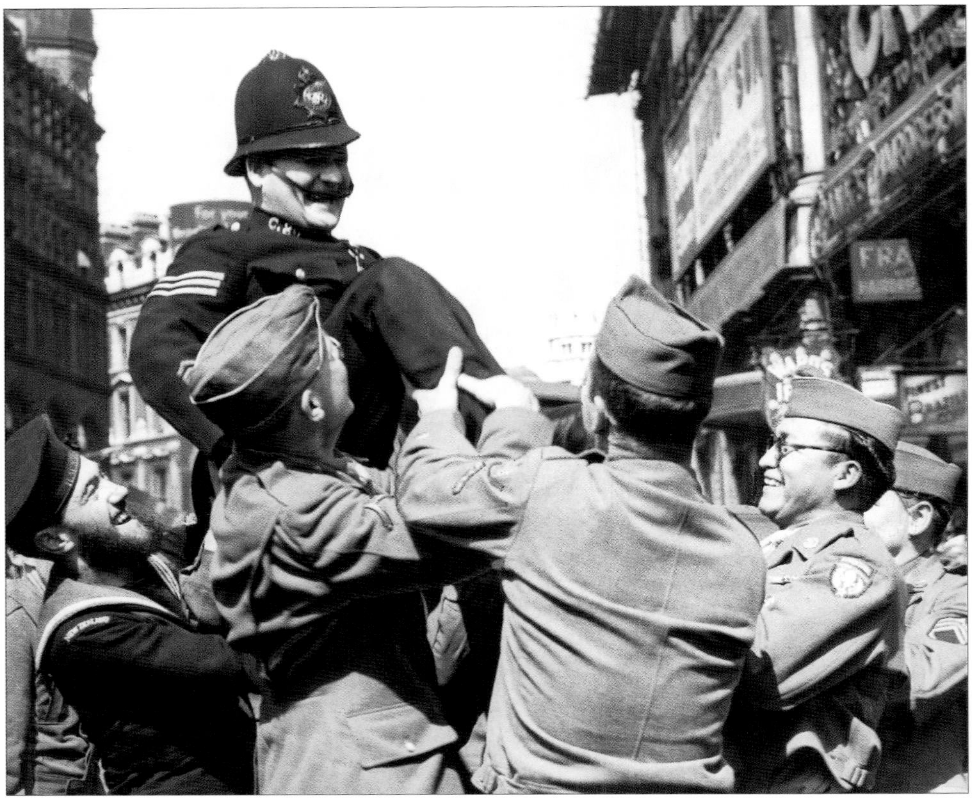

WANTED
PAPER RAGS BONES FOR MUNITIONS
AMERICAN RED CROSS
RAINBOW CORNER
ALDWYCH
EVERY WEDNESDAY
Good Taste Demands
HöVIS
Not Just Brown

Celebrations

This was the scene in Piccadilly at three o'clock in the morning. Celebrations for VJ Day were, if anything, even more unrestrained than those for VE Day. It was the end to a war which for people in Britain had lasted just twenty days short of six years.

Victory Day

Above: On 8th June 1946 there was an opportunity for formal celebrations to give thanks to everyone who contributed to the war effort. A 21,000 strong parade of British and Allied forces as well as civilian workers stretched for twenty miles. Here the King takes the salute at the march-past.

Page 86: The King and Queen, with Queen Mary, Princess Margaret and Princess Elizabeth (behind the King), watch a fly-past by 300 RAF aircraft on Victory Day.

Page 87: Contingents of military from the Commonwealth march along Whitehall in the Victory Day parade.

Opposite: The crowds gathered in Trafalgar Square on VJ Day - everyone has their own way of celebrating!

WORMS EYE VIEW
THE FUNNIEST PLAY IN TOWN

Prime Ministers in war and peace

Above: Side by side on the saluting base on Victory Day, 8th June 1946, are Clement Attlee, Prime Minister of the day, alongside Winston Churchill, the man who had led Britain through five years of war.

Left: Commonwealth leaders also attended the Victory Day parade. Here are Mackenzie King, Prime Minister of Canada (left) and Field Marshal Smuts, the South African PM.

Opposite top: Field Marshal Montgomery, now Viscount of Alamein, in his car at the head of the four-mile-long mechanised column in the parade. Here the car sets off from Clarence Gate, Regent's Park.

Opposite below: Montgomery at the head of the vehicles in the Victory Day parade is welcomed in the East End among people living in an area which continues to bear the scars of German bombing. Many people were in temporary housing a year into the peace and many would never return, settling instead in the areas to which they had been evacuated.

Commonwealth troops

Troops from India march in the parade. There were representatives from all the nations who fought for the Allies, as well as men and women who gave their efforts to defend the Home Front.

FUNNIEST PLAY IN TOWN
MS EYE VIEW

Victory fireworks at the heart of London

The end of the celebrations on Victory Day 1946 - a huge firework display watched by the King and Queen and hundreds of thousands of spectators. Coloured fountains played from fire-tugs and fireworks shot up from barges moored in the Thames.

ACKNOWLEDGEMENTS

The photographs in this book are from the archives of the *Daily Mail*. Particular thanks to Steve Torrington, Dave Sheppard, Brian Jackson, Alan Pinnock, Paul Rossiter, Richard Jones and all the staff.

Thanks also to Cliff Salter, Richard Betts, Liz Balmer, Peter Wright, Trevor Bunting and Simon Taylor.

Design by John Dunne.